Jacky Newcomb is the UK's leading expert on the after-life, having dedicated her life to the subject. She is a *Sunday Times* bestselling author with numerous awards to her name, a regular columnist for *Take a Break*'s *Fate & Fortune* magazine, and is a regular on ITV's *This Morning*, and C5's *Live with Gabby*. Jacky has also appeared on *Lorraine* and *The Alan Titchmarsh Show*, among others.

Also by Jacky Newcomb:

Dogs in Heaven

Dogs in Heaven

and Other Animals

Extraordinary stories of animals
reaching out from the other side

Jacky Newcomb

Harper
True *Fate*

Some names have been changed to protect
the privacy of the story tellers.

HarperTrueFate
An imprint of HarperCollins*Publishers*
1 London Bridge Street,
London SE1 9GF

www.harpertrue.com
www.harpercollins.co.uk

First published by HarperTrueFate 2015

© Jacky Newcomb 2015

Jacky Newcomb asserts the moral right to
be identified as the author of this work

A catalogue record of this book is
available from the British Library

ISBN: 978-0-00-810519-8

Chapter 1

Visits from the Other Side

Animals have always been important in my life, and, I suspect, in yours too. They bring us comfort and joy, watch over us, keep us safe and keep us company. Our pets are happy to listen to our problems and are always on our side. Your cat doesn't care if your clothes are in fashion, and your dog doesn't really mind what you talk to him about. You could live in a shed or a mansion, have old furniture or surround yourself with the very latest in interior design. Your pets really aren't interested and don't judge you either way.

The pets that have come into my life have often appeared by coincidence, or maybe through some magical or mystical means. Their lives with me have continued along in the same way, and it has fascinated me how closely our pets become entwined with our lives and our hearts; so much so that after they pass away, that connection seems to remain unbroken.

It seems obvious to me that, having spent our lives sharing such unrestricted love, animals and humans have a very deep connection. Doesn't it make sense that the relationship would exist on a deeper level than the physical one we share in our earthly bodies? Over the years I've written about many of these connections: contact that happens in a psychic way; a communication that exists separate to the body; a magnetic draw that endures long after the body of either party has died. A dog is a man's best friend both during and after life.

When my rescue dog Lady was euthanised, the guilt I felt was enormous. I know you'll understand when I say that it didn't help me to know that I had made the decision to end her life through love. I still felt bad about it. Afterwards I cried for several days until I had the most extraordinary experience. One night she appeared to me in a very vivid dream.

The little black-and-tan dog we'd chosen from the rescue centre was already several years old by the time she made her home with us; she could have been aged anywhere from three to seven years. We'd never known her as a puppy, yet in the dream she was a pretty little pup and full of energy. She bounced around in front of me and although she didn't speak, I felt a message coming from her. It was just as if she were saying to me, 'Look, Mum, I'm fine! Look how well I am now, look how much vigour and vitality I have!'

Lady was surrounded by other dogs we'd owned as a family over the years. This friendly group of dogs had all presented themselves as puppies in the dream. If dogs could smile, this was what they were doing. I recognised dogs we'd owned when I was a child, and others that had belonged to my sisters and their families. They were all there in the dream! Only one was missing. Candy, a female Jack Russell that had bitten me as a child, was not with the other companions we'd loved so much. I don't know where she was, but maybe bad dogs go somewhere else. I felt great comfort in knowing that the dogs were all together, and after this very real dream my guilt went away for good. I shared this full story (and others) in my book *An Angel Held My Hand*. It was important to me to know that Lady had carried on after death. Her life hadn't ended when her body died.

My cat Tigger, a fat ginger tom, was friends with her too, and in one of those bizarre coincidences he has just jumped up onto my desk as I write this. As he looks up at the screen, it's as if he is showing his approval of his friend's immortalisation in this book! How do they know?

Was my experience a dream or something more? I've always believed that it was a real visit from my dog's spirit after she passed over to the heaven side of life. It was clear and vivid; the colours were bright and memorable, the experience real and true, and I've never forgotten it, even after all these years.

My post bag has yielded many such stories over time. Lots of folk have experienced contact of some sort from their pets once they have crossed over. You may have read about how our human loved ones do this (and you can find out more about this phenomenon in some of my other books), but did you know that animals continue to exist after the death of their physical bodies too? It's true! The spirit of our pet lingers, as they want to reassure us that they did not die – at least, not in the way we think.

Dogs, cats, horses, hamsters, rabbits: I've been sent true-life stories about all of these animals and more. Don't forget birds! Birds continue after life too. They all appear in vivid dreams from time to time, like the one I had myself, but also make themselves known by bringing familiar scents or sounds to their owners – just popping back to say hello. Sometimes they appear in intense waking visions. That love from our pets continues after death.

We've always been a family of pet lovers. Moggy was my first ginger tom cat. He lived with us when I was a teenager, and he would sleep on my bed at night. Cats always understand you, even when no one else does, and a teenager always needs a friend!

Moggy was a real hunter and the house was always full of dead things. One night he caught a live mouse and my sisters rescued it. Many years later they explained how they had shut the mouse in the bathroom and played with it for about an hour. Days later I remember waking up to hear scratching noises in my bedroom. I saw something run across the floor, but when I yelled out for my mum and dad to check, they told me I must be having a nightmare. Apparently, my sisters – who shared the bedroom next door – just looked at each other guiltily. The mouse (as mice do) had escaped from the bathroom, but they had been too frightened to tell anyone. It was now running freely around the house!

I think the worst moment came when I woke up one night to hear crunching on the landing. Moggy had caught a baby rabbit. Even though I was now awake, it was still a horrible nightmare. Moggy growled protectively over his catch as my dad chased him out of the house. Ugh! But cats are cats, and I loved him just the same. I was devastated when he died, and a visit from the other side would have reassured me so much.

When my husband and I were first married we decided to get a cat of our own. A house never seemed like a home without one. I missed my old tom cat and we chose another ginger tom. We called him Charlie. He used to skit about the floor in a bizarre zigzag movement and I nearly tripped over him several times. One day he ran into the path of my poor husband, who fell awkwardly on the floor. Unfortunately, John's shoe caught Charlie's back foot and the cat let out a terrible screech. We rushed him to the vet – Charlie had broken his back leg.

I'll never forget how he looked with that plaster on. His leg had been bandaged straight out and he dragged it behind him. But we needn't have worried; he coped very well. For six weeks he continued his crazy antics, except that he would clomp his leg on the door frames as he ran through!

Charlie was a bruiser with attitude. He never sat on your lap and you always felt that he stayed around because he had nothing better to do. When he wanted feeding he would come up to us and rub himself up against our legs or purr loudly in my ear. If we didn't pay attention quickly enough, we had about one whole minute before he would start to get angry about it.

Stage two would involve him patting us with his paw, but the purring would have stopped. He would keep nudging us and walk towards the kitchen as if to say, 'Come on, then – follow me, you stupid owners!'

God help you if you missed the second signal. Stage three was painful. He would jump up and bite us and then run for it! We did learn never to shout at him, because he always got his own back. Charlie used to hide and wait for the perfect moment. His favourite place was at the bottom of the stairs, and when we walked down he would pounce on us as if we were his prey! Several times he drew blood ... It hurt!

When we were first married we owned a cheap pine and canvas sofa. Charlie would run along the underside, clinging onto the canvas. Backwards and forwards he would go, and you had to watch out for your tights. We kept him for many years, and when we moved house I became pregnant. We were worried about how we might cope with a cat and a baby in the house, but sadly Charlie got run over on the main road shortly before I had my first baby. He had been aggressive and mean, but we loved him dearly and again I cried a lot when he died.

One night several months later I woke up to feel the familiar padding of his paws on the bed and I forgot for a moment that he had died. When I sat up in bed I could even see the circular space where he'd been sitting, but of course he was only there in spirit. It was as if he had come to say goodbye. This was my first experience of animal contact from beyond the grave.

Ten years later we were burgled in that house and so we bought a dog. But Brandy kept running away, so we had to get her rehomed by the RSPCA. I cried again – a lot – but buying a dog at this time (a bois-terous collie cross) had been a big mistake; it was really stressful. Even though Brandy was still alive I grieved her loss – I recall crying every day for over six weeks after she went. I vowed never to have any more pets, but, you guessed it … several years later we picked up two rescue kittens.

I found the first one in a local pet shop. You could still buy kittens that way then, and I was horrified to see this little black cat, dirty and scruffy-looking, curled up in a small rabbit-sized cage.

My husband had not been keen on getting any more pets, so I secretly arranged for the kitten to be collected while he was at work. I emailed him a picture of a black kitten with the message: 'I live with you now' (pretty mean of me, wasn't it?). I was hoping that once he came home and saw this fluffy bundle he would fall in love with it, and to a certain extent he did! I gave John permission to name the cat (another sneaky technique). He was a long-haired black kitten with a white patch under his chin – John called him DJ, because it looked like he was wearing a dinner jacket. He grew up to be a very attractive cat indeed.

DJ had been living with us for a week before I picked up the second kitten. Portia was a tiny female tabby and she never left my side. She was timid and shy and yet loved attention. If she couldn't sit on my lap she would curl herself around my shoulders. Both cats were gentle and sweet. DJ was happy to be fussed over and would sit on your lap if you put him there.

Both cats were also happy to be played with. When my two daughters were small they would often dress the cats up in dolls' clothes and push them around in their pushchairs. The cats would just purr loudly! They were very forgiving and loved the attention.

Dogs in Heaven

One day, the girls were following the cats around pretending to be cats themselves. It was a fun game. Georgina, my youngest, was curled up on the sofa next to Portia, who was sleeping, and Charlotte was mimicking DJ, who was bouncing around the furniture. DJ walked through the lounge and into the kitchen with Charlotte following closely behind. DJ jumped onto the kitchen worktop to climb onto the top of the fridge, and Charlotte, making sure that no one could see her, grabbed a kitchen stool and jumped right up behind him. We discovered what she had done just a few seconds later when we heard the almighty crash! Loud screams could be heard from the kitchen.

'I've broken my arm – take me to the hospital!' she screamed.

And so she had! Kittens often get themselves into trouble. It seemed that children pretending to be kittens did the same thing.

Because we lived on a main road we kept the cats in the house most of the time, but we did have a run made for them in the garden. In the summer we put them outside and they would happily catch flies or just sunbathe on the tiered stand that John had made for them in their run. One day, I popped outside to bring the cats in and the door to the run was open – and worse, the side gate to the garden was also ajar.

We never saw the cats again, even though we searched for six weeks or more. I telephoned everyone I knew and had many people searching the roads and gardens in the area. It was a terrible thing. We walked the entire village and looked under every hedgerow. Our neighbours were having a lot of building work done at the time and often had lorries parked outside their house with the backs open. I liked to think that maybe the cats had climbed in and fallen asleep in the back. I dreamt that when the driver reached his destination the cats ran out and were immediately found by a cat lover who took them in and loved them the way that I did. It was how I coped with their loss for a very long time. The grief was once again unbearable, and as before I vowed never to get another pet.

I guess, like in the childhood film *The Incredible Journey* where three pets find their way home to their owners after they have moved house, I always hoped mine would find me again. But there was no happy ending to this story. Cats are special and find a place in our hearts, which is hard to replace.

It was many years again before I felt ready to buy another cat, because the heartache of losing these special creatures was too hard to bear. But being without them is almost as bad, so finally I succumbed. I began dreaming of a new kitten entering our lives. It was as if it was psychically ordained somehow. The dream would occur regularly, almost as if the kitten had been born and was waiting for us some-where. I mentioned it to my husband, who immediately said, 'No way!' (and who could blame him); but I was undeterred. I began ringing up various rescue centres, and bought a collar and even some cat food in preparation!

My youngest daughter also had a dream and came in to see me one morning confidently saying, 'Mum, I've seen the cat. It's a male ginger kitten and it was chasing a butterfly.' I felt sure she was right.

I begged my husband to take me to the RSPCA and we went together. Nothing felt right, though, and I was gutted when they told us we would be unable to take a kitten home immediately. I just burst into tears! Now, I'm not one to cry – in fact, I NEVER cry – unless, it seems, a pet is involved. They asked us to select a kitten, but in my mind it was too late – if we couldn't take one home that day, I didn't want one from them at all. John and the girls went back to the car while I pointed to a female tabby kitten. 'That one's fine,' I said, with no emotion.

I was so embarrassed as the tears just kept falling down my face. All I wanted to do was go home, but I had to stay and fill in all the forms. A couple of people walked in behind me and I tried to hide my face. I knew they were wondering why I was crying, but I guess it was all the frustration of losing my kittens before. The memory just came flooding back and it was too much to handle. I wanted a kitten and I wanted it now.

The next day I telephoned the RSPCA and apologised for my behaviour but told them I had changed my mind. The kitten had been beautiful but she wasn't our cat. Later that day I had a telephone call from the Cats Protection League. 'Sorry I've taken so long to get back to you, Mrs Newcomb, but I've been away on holiday. We have several kittens in your area, including a couple of ginger tomcats, and they are ready now. Would you like to see them?'

I couldn't believe it! I knew that our cat was among them, so we planned to visit later in the day. We rushed to the local garden centre to pick up a travel basket and placed it ready in the back of the car, then drove straight over to the 'foster mother' who was caring for the mother and her four kittens. They were eleven weeks old and neither of the male toms was particularly small. Memories of Charlie and his broken leg came flooding back and I was glad that these were a little bigger; it would be safer, I figured.

One of the male cats had a sore on his neck and was being treated with antibiotics. He was lovely but not ready to be taken away yet. My eldest daughter fell in love with the smallest female kitten and cried that we couldn't have two. 'Pick her up,' I suggested, but the kitten just bit her and scrambled right over her head, scratching her arm on the way up to her basket. My youngest daughter had no such difficulties. She had already seen the ginger tomcat in her dream and just pointed quietly to the kitten sitting calmly in the corner.

'That's the one, Mum', she said.

I picked him up and we carried him into the foster mother's house where we signed all the forms and handed over our donation. We were able to take him straight home. This was our cat, he'd been shown to us in a dream and we knew it was right! We named him Tigger in the car on the way home, and as I carried him into our house I spotted a butterfly in the garden – the first one of the year – and I recalled my daughter seeing the cat playing with a butterfly in her dream. A strange coincidence, or just another sign? Who could tell?

Tigger gave a new lease of life to our elderly dog Lady. They took about a week to become friends and then happily chased each other around the house. Tigger grew into the most beautiful cat. He always came when we called him and slept in a shopping basket in the kitchen at night with Lady (they had one each!).

Fortunately, Tigger prefers to be inside the house, and if he does venture outside he rarely leaves the garden. It's as if he knows how much I would worry if he went too far away. Thankfully, we live on a safe road. Each time we've moved house you can guarantee that top of our list of house requirements has been that it be safe for the cat! The trouble is that pets have a much shorter life than we humans do. If you own many pets over your lifetime it means that you're going to lose a few too. Mystical experiences of animals coming to say goodbye after death can bring great comfort. When this happened to me I felt I healed quicker, but when the experiences didn't come the grief went on for much longer. Luckily, we have Tigger still. He is ten now!

Chapter 2

Man's Best Friend

My readers have experienced amazing animal connections of their own. One lady wrote to me about her dog Sophie, who was nearly twenty years old. Sophie's legs had started to give way and her owner knew it was time to make the decision to let her go. Like me, and many others, she found the decision-making process challenging. One day she asked the angels if they would bring her a sign that she was doing the right thing. The woman was surprised when two pieces of music came on the radio, one after the other. The first was 'Gabriel's Oboe' by Ennio Morricone (and Gabriel, of course, is the name of the archangel) and the other was a song about heaven.

She decided to go ahead and take the dog to the vet, but on the day she asked her son to accompany her. When they arrived, her son took the dog in while she sat in the car with tears running down her face. Then she saw the most amazing sight. Sophie was running. She seemed to run right out of the vet surgery wall and across the car park, and then she disappeared. Sophie may have finished with her physical body, but her spirit body was up and ready to begin her new life. Although still sad, the family found great comfort in knowing that their pet was now free of her pain and clearly happy once more. Isn't that amazing? I know I would have found comfort in the experience too.

In a similar story, a man had taken his sick dog to the vet, and the vet had decided to keep the pet in overnight for observation. That night the man was sleeping at home in what he described as a big bed, with his wife and the family's two other dogs. He was woken by the sound of 'something' running down the hallway; although he couldn't see anything, he felt this 'something' jump up onto the bed. The other dogs noticed it too and both of them stared at the empty spot. Sadly, the next morning the vet called to say that the poorly dog had passed away during the night, but the family will never forget that their pet came back one last time to say goodbye.

This next story is from Lottie. Her dad doesn't have brothers but he did have a very close connection to Lottie's mum's brother, and years earlier the siblings had owned a dog called Snowy.

When Lottie's uncle died of cancer, her dad found it very hard; he'd lost a friend and a brother at the same time. A few weeks after his death, Lottie's mum was getting ready for work and was making a cup of tea. Lottie's dad was drifting in and out of sleep when her mum shouted up the stairs to him, 'Do you want tea?' Yet Lottie's dad swears to this day that she shouted, 'Who's got the dog?' Her dad immediately heard the response in his head: 'I have him, I have Snowy,' as clear as day in the voice of Lottie's recently departed uncle!

Sadly, Lottie's dad was so freaked out by this experience that he jumped out of bed and had to look around his room – he didn't go back to sleep! I'm sure his brother-in-law was trying to bring him comfort by letting him know that he'd met up with a special pet from his past; he was trying to let him know that they were both alive and well in their new heavenly home! Isn't that a strange one?

This next story has various spooky qualities about it – but in a good way! Sister Mary, a nun, wrote to tell me how much she enjoyed my books and to share her own experiences. She had owned a special Hearing Dog for the Deaf. Being profoundly deaf and unable to use hearing aids, her life prior to having her four-legged helper had been a big challenge. Trixie was a hairless Chinese crested cross Japanese Chin; a lovable, cheeky girl who taught her owner lots about life and, yes, about God too! They built up a fantastic relationship and in many ways the dog became Mary's soul mate. Trixie seemed to know what her owner was thinking, and even acted as a bit of a stress-buster. Mary says her tinnitus drove her round the bend, but Trixie always kept her calm.

The first sign, Mary realised, that dogs can see more than we can came when she drove her dog and mother to visit her father's grave; it was her first visit since receiving Trixie. As she drove into the cemetery, Trixie sat up, looked round and started crying. Mary's mum told Trixie that it was okay, and that the people at the cemetery were asleep and were fine, Trixie stopped crying and was happy again.

Another time, when Mary was praying, she suddenly saw her pet gazing intently at an icon of Jesus. Mary asked, 'Jesus, are you in the room with us?' She knew he was – it was amazing the way that little dog gazed. Trixie loved going to Mass and visiting churches. She was even taken up to Holy Communion so that she wasn't left in the pew on her own. Many times, as Mary received the host, the little dog did a sort of bow. Others witnessed this too.

Trixie became terminally ill at the end of February 2005. Her heart had become enlarged and she passed with a massive heart attack. About three minutes later Mary was flooded with a feeling of sheer bliss. She says it was almost too much to take as she immediately felt that Trixie was back with her in spirit. She was letting her owner know she was well, young and free. Mary felt her dog had conveyed a sense of awe and wonder at what was happening to her and she felt grateful for loving her and letting her go.

Mary told me: 'I know that gorgeous little dog of mine asked God if she could let me know she was fine. I treasure that so much and it helped me in the unbearable weeks ahead.' Not only had she lost her faithful companion – as a Hearing Dog, Trixie went everywhere with Mary – it was also as if Mary had suddenly become deaf once more.

A week later, on the Saturday evening, Mary flung her sandals on top of each other in the room where she kept her computer. The next morning, before going to Mass, she went in to get the sandals and nearly passed out. Instead of being on top of each other, the sandals were now side by side, and Trixie's favourite treat, a Rancho, was sitting neatly in front of them. Several years later Trixie appeared in the flesh. As her owner walked into the house the dog was sitting in front of the fire looking at her! Trixie, it seemed, had never gone very far away.

Mary explained that after her mother died she was also around a lot – and she made it clear that she had Trixie with her. Trixie sounds like she was a very special dog in life and in death, and I'm pleased to say that several months later Mary was given a replacement Hearing Dog.

Lisa was also kind enough to share her experience with me. She told me that, a few weeks after her dog Dibley passed over, she had a dream in which her late mother was taking the dog for a walk. In the dream her mum told Lisa that she would now look after Dibley and that she wasn't to worry because they were together. Isn't that wonderful? I find it so comforting to hear that our pets are being taken care of in heaven.

Julie wrote to tell me about her unusual experience regarding her pet rabbit. She loved him very much and found his passing very challenging indeed. She told me that after he died she cried over her loss for many weeks. Then something magical happened. Julie said that she dreamed of him several times, as if he was trying to let her know he was still around. She also saw him popping his nose out from under the sofa, just like he used to when he was alive!

When pets visit us in dreams they tend to look especially healthy and well. We notice this all the more because they may have been ill just before they passed away. It's hard to see a sick pet suffer, but it's certainly comforting to see them well again when they are in the afterlife.

Roxanne's mum and dad got a puppy when Roxanne was only a month old. She grew up with the dog until the age of ten, when her pet sadly passed away. One day, a couple of years later, Roxanne remembers waking up in bed, and straight ahead of her was their dog, Bell. She says the two of them gazed at each other for a few moments before she rubbed her eyes; when she looked back Bell was gone. Although she was a young girl at the time, Roxanne wasn't scared at all – she says she knew Bell was coming back to say hi because she was so greatly missed.

Katie's aunt and uncle moved to Spain a few years ago, but their dog visited her in a dream a few days before he died. It's not unusual for the spirit of a pet (or human) to appear in this way in the days or hours before they die. Katie says this dog was the only one she ever trusted, as the family had owned him since she was eight.

The dog's name was Z; he was a Border Collie. When Katie's aunt and uncle first got him she did not like the dog, especially when he used to jump up at her. Later the pair became friends and she was happy to cuddle with him. She missed the dog so much after they moved to Spain, but then a few months ago Z came to her in the dream. She stroked him in the dream and when she woke up she emailed her aunt to ask if Z was okay. Her aunt said yes, but sadly, a few days later, Z died. He had clearly bonded with Katie as much as with his owners, and took the opportunity to say goodbye before he left for the afterlife. It's sad when this happens, but as I've seen in my own life, when pets say goodbye it makes the passing so much easier!

When people see their deceased pets unexpectedly, and they automatically reach out to stroke them and feel their presence, they then realise that what they are seeing is real. After an old family dog, Suzie, died at my mother's house, the whole family still felt her greet us at the door when we visited. She was a scruffy rescue dog, medium sized, with a camel-coloured coat. She had an ugly tail that curled around – we used to call it a piggy-tail! Yet Suzie spent her life being grateful to her family. You could tell she was just happy to be alive, and we loved her so much.

After she passed away her spirit remained at the house. You could sense her circling around and feel her tail wagging against your leg. Sometimes I could see her as a faded-out shape; it lasted for just a second or two. Far from being scary, it was actually a wonderful feeling. It continued for several months, and then she just disappeared. I always felt she wanted to stick around to make sure we were all okay before she left.

Three years exactly after their Yorkshire Terrier Ben passed away, Karen heard the noise her dog used to make when it was dreaming. She immediately turned to her partner and said, 'Did you hear that?' Her partner had heard it too!

Rachel told me that even a year after her dog passed on she would still hear him bark sometimes. She recalled once seeing him sitting by the door, waiting to go out, in the same way he did when he was alive. She believes that pets do stick around after they have passed on, and I do too … for a while at least! Janice wrote to me with a similar story. A year after her neighbour's dog passed away she would still see him waiting at the school bus stop as he did every day when he was alive. Animal spirits tend to follow the same rituals they had when alive, and this familiarity brings great comfort to the pet and their owner. Sometimes the pet comes back to help us, but other times I believe they like to hang around for their own benefit. They slip backwards and forwards between this side and the next until they feel ready to move on for good.

I think we build up a bank of signs and sounds relating to our animals, so that when they pass we recognise them easily. My current cat's bell has a very unique sound (he has several bells attached to his collar), and one day recently my husband and I were out for a walk. I heard Tigger's bell and said to my husband that I knew it was him. The way he trots along, it makes a very unique chime. My husband was dismissive, as the area we were walking in was some distance from our home and we didn't know it as part of our cat's normal territory. I decided to call the cat nonetheless, and sure enough Tigger immediately jumped over a fence and happily followed us home, rushing inside to be fed.

Now I wonder, if he'd been dead and I'd heard that exact same sound, would anyone have believed me when I'd said it was him? Trust your instincts! You know your own pet better than anyone. If you sense, hear or smell your pet after it's passed on, then you're probably experiencing a real spirit visit. It is exactly what it seems to be; as the old saying goes, the most likely explanation is probably the correct one. Deborah says her cat had a very unique mew, and after it died she regularly heard it calling out to her. Even her husband, a non-believer, heard it.

Anne also shared her experience with me. She told me that when her parents' dog died a few months before her dad himself passed on, he was so upset. But, Anne says, since her father's passing, she's had an unusual experience that lets her know the dog is okay. One night she awoke to see a dog and a person walking and running around her bedroom. She says the experience seemed so real that for a brief moment she wondered if it was her own dog (which was still living), before she remembered that he was fast asleep in the kitchen downstairs!

Had the dog appeared with its heavenly guardian? It does seem likely. Numerous experiences people have shared with me seem to indicate that pets are taken care of on the other side. Sometimes they appear in spirit visitations with human loved ones who've also passed on. It's as if they want us to know that everyone is being looked after, and that pets can visit or stay with humans they know, or be with other family pets that have also passed over. They are all taken care of by angelic helpers in heaven! I know it sounds crazy, but people have shared such experiences with me over and over again, and I see no reason to doubt their stories.

One man woke to see his deceased pet standing by the bed. He said he spoke to the dog and told him how much the family loved him and missed him. That's all he recalls before he fell back to sleep. Another man, who'd lost his cat four years earlier, dreamt that the cat climbed up his leg and sat upon his shoulder. He recalls sensing the pet around him previously, but this was the most vivid experience to date.

One young woman explained that after her cat passed away it kept visiting her in dreams too. But she worried because the cat appeared sick in the dreams, just as it was before it passed over. After my father passed on he appeared in some dreams to show us just how ill he had been. I felt it was almost an apology, a sort of 'sorry I had to leave you, but as you can see I was very unwell'. I'd recommend that this woman acknowledge this, maybe even saying out loud (talking to a photo of the late cat), 'It's okay, we understand, and it was okay to pass away when you did.' This will probably stop the dreams, if she is concerned about them. If she is really lucky the pet will visit again, this time showing her how well he has become.

One cat visited her owner again and again after she'd sadly passed away from cancer. The owner and his partner were much attached to their pet and kept her ashes along with a photograph in their bedroom. Two years after the passing, the owner woke up several times over numerous days as he felt the cat's paws walking over his leg. He even saw the bedding move, but says that after sitting up in bed and looking around, he couldn't see anything! Cats do this when they are alive too, of course. One gentleman wrote that every night he would wake up after feeling little paws walking all over him. His cat appeared to be fast asleep on the bed, so he assumed it must be spirits trying to annoy him. After several frustrated and restless nights he set up his camcorder to record what was happening. What he caught on film completely stunned him. His sneaky cat would paw all over him and then, as soon as he sat up in bed to check what was going on, it would lie back down again and pretend to be asleep! Isn't that funny? Of course, that cat wasn't a spirit, but I couldn't resist including the story in this book for you.

Julia's beautiful Amazon parrot Connie had passed away some eighteen months before when she unexpectedly appeared in a dream. The bird was rolling around and playing, having her tummy and wings tickled, and saying the words, 'Elmo loves you,' before getting back into her cage. As she did so Julia could see inside the cage, and another bird was right there beside her. Julia says the green bird next to Connie was slightly out of focus in the dream, so she couldn't see it clearly.

Dogs in Heaven

Then one day, three weeks after the dream, Julia found 'Elmo' by accident in a garden centre when she was out with her two-year-old son Archie. Elmo is a gorgeous Hahn's macaw, and he instantly bonded with them both there and then in the shop. The new bird now lives in the giant cage once owned by the late Connie, and yes, he says, 'Elmo loves you,' and blows kisses to his human family! Strangely, when Connie was alive she didn't roll around as she did in the dream, but the new bird does. Julia firmly believes that Connie brought them their new pet by sharing her message and arranging things from the other side!

TV Presenter Anthea Turner is a dear friend of mine and she kindly gave me permission to share her story with you here. Anthea always loved dogs, and when she worked on the children's television programme *Blue Peter* in the early 1990s, she always requested to work on any features that included the show's dog, Bonnie. Bonnie was a Golden Retriever who appeared on the programme from 1986 to 1999, and although the *Blue Peter* pets had their own carers, Anthea spent as much time with Bonnie as she could.

A few years later, Anthea and her new husband had the opportunity to buy their own Golden Retriever pup. The partner of her make-up artist at the GMTV studio in London was a breeder, who was based in Cornwall. They decided to meet half-way at the Devonshire home of another friend, TV presenter Noel Edmonds. In May 1999 the couple fell in love with a gorgeous pup with the kennel name of Excavator; they cleverly decided to call him Digger! Now Digger needed a friend, a buddy, so they picked up a second pup as well, and naturally they called him Buddie!

Sadly, Anthea was unable to have children of her own, so the dogs became her children. The new pups quickly settled in and everyone adored the new family members. Both dogs had great characters, with Buddie being the quieter of the two. Digger was cheekier and often got his brother into trouble! The two of them loved charging around together and had a very happy life. Digger lived until he was ten years old, and passed away from cancer. Anthea was devastated.

As Buddie got older he developed problems too. He had a lot of issues with his hip, and Anthea did everything she could to prolong his life. Then one day she knew she could no longer delay the inevitable. As every pet owner knows, you look into your pet's eyes and it's like they reach out to you and say, 'Come on, Mum/Dad, it's time to let go. It's time for me to go home.' When you've lived with an animal their whole life you know everything there is to know about them, you communicate in many ways, and Buddie's old body was tired. He was ready to join his brother.

Dogs in Heaven

My friend had recently split up with her husband and felt even more devastated at the double blow. With her sister coming along to the vet for moral support, she sat with Buddie, crying and saying goodbye. She held him and stroked him one last time as he quietly slipped away.

Buddie had developed what Anthea calls an 'old man woof' in his last few months or so. It was very distinctive. The morning after a restless night, she was working on her computer in the office at home when she heard Buddie's distinctive bark, loud and clear. Anthea was startled, but wondered if maybe she was hearing things. Then her housekeeper walked in from the other room. She'd heard Buddie too! There was no mistake.

Anthea felt that her beloved pet was just popping back to say goodbye – it was as if he was reassuring her that he was okay. She now firmly believes that there is an afterlife, and knows that one day she'll be with her dogs once more.

Sharon's partner had a similar experience. He lived with his mother and his dog Noodles until the dog passed over earlier this year. The couple now live together, but on a recent visit to his mother's house he heard his late pet bark just seconds before he opened the door. His mum had been fast asleep and not heard a thing!

Have you ever heard the sound of a pet after it has passed away? We're used to watching TV programmes

Jacky Newcomb

that cover afterlife phenomena – maybe spooky howling or the flapping of wings from some unseen creature. Yet the reality is that these afterlife sounds are more likely to come from someone (or something) known to you. Love is the strongest connection to the afterlife. The bond is what draws the realms together. Those we love – human and animal – long to stay connected after death. My books are full of such stories, featuring humans reaching out from the afterlife to reassure their loved ones that life has continued for them (though in a different way). The same is true of animal contact. For some humans, their closest earthly friend is a pet; that connection cannot be severed even after death. The higher realms have never been keener to give permission for that afterlife connection to be made.

I loved the story from the book by Scott S. Smith, *The Soul of Your Pet: Evidence for the Survival of Animals After Death*. A professor of veterinary medicine shared an experience from her time in private practice. It happened one day when making a call to see to a sick horse. Following on from her examination, she advised the owners that the horse's condition was infectious. She suggested the owners separate the horse from its companion, a white horse standing nearby.

The horse's owners seemed confused, as the vet was pointing at nothing. There was no white horse.

Dogs in Heaven

The vet described the white horse's markings and couldn't understand why the couple couldn't see it. Spookily, the owners had lost a white horse with these same markings just months earlier; the vet was seeing their dead horse! Maybe the white horse had popped back to comfort its sick friend. What's interesting about this story is the fact that the vet had been the one to see the horse, not the owners; no one could accuse them of 'wishful thinking'! This story did make the hairs stand up on the back of my neck … but in a good way, of course.

Alice got in touch with me to share a very moving experience. She felt as if she had been woken one night. She switched on the light to discover that, sadly, her cat had quietly passed away beside her. She felt that her pet's soul had reached out one last time to say goodbye as it slipped away, and I'm sure she was right.

There is a difference between a normal dream about a pet and a visitation (real spirit visits from your pet's soul in heaven). If the contact happens while you are asleep, the vision has certain qualities about it that make it easy to recognise. The real visitation experience is very vivid, as was my own when my dog Lady visited me. You'll be completely aware that your own body is asleep during the encounter and that your pet has 'died'. You may talk to your pet and they may communicate with you. I've never experienced a pet talking like a human by moving its mouth; pets seem to speak using a sort of telepathy instead, mind-to-mind contact during our sleeping hours. The communication might come as words, but more likely your pet will transfer a complete message or idea to your mind. For example, you may get a real sense of your pet's well-being rather than hearing it say, 'Hey, man, I'm okay!' You'll feel your animal's happiness and health.

Your pet may seem young, vibrant or full of energy. They might demonstrate their state of well-being by running or jumping about or appearing particularly shiny or fluffy. Their eyes may sparkle (indicating good health), and of course they will let you know how happy they are to see you and greet you fondly.

To dream of an animal (an ordinary dream) is very different. You might still wake and feel that the experience was important, but that could be because some sort of symbolism has been shown in the dream. A good dream dictionary will help you, or you can look up traditional meanings of animal dreams on the Internet. To dream of a dog, for example, might mean that you value someone's loyalty and companionship, or maybe that they are *leading* you. Horses are exciting but also unpredictable; they represent transportation, helping us to get from one place to the next. Cats are independent and more than a little mysterious. Mice are timid, so when they appear in a dream it might show low self-esteem or similar. Dreaming of a tortoise might be a sign of longevity, or perhaps having (or carrying) everything you need on your back. You get the idea!

Have you had a dream about animals or a dream visitation from an animal spirit? A dream and a visitation are the difference between reading a book and meeting someone in a bar. You get the sense that what happened while you slept was a real one-to-one connection, a real contact encounter

So why do they come? Sometimes pets want to warn us about something coming up in the future, but usually it's simply to let us know they are okay. They want to reassure us or just pop by to say hello. Knowing they are okay is really helpful in the grieving process.

One man dreamt that his pet came to warn him to stop smoking. He was a big smoker, so the pet was suggesting that throat cancer might be a likely outcome if he continued. Scary, but helpful. I don't recall my dog giving me any predictions about my own life, but I would have been happy if she had – as long as it wasn't too late to do something about it, of course.

Karen was kind enough to tell me about her own cat's experience. She explained that Clyde was put to sleep last June, and naturally she was heartbroken. It was more than that, though; she felt 'mad' and 'inconsolable', she says, mainly because she never

---

got to say goodbye. She'd taken her cat to the vet so he could just check over the pet's lungs. The next day Karen was at work when she got a phone call to say that Clyde had needed to be put to sleep, as he had an incurable lung disease and it was kinder to let him go while he was under anaesthetic.

Poor Karen was in complete shock – she had been expecting her cat home the next day. A big part of her felt angry that she never got to say goodbye in person and tell him that she loved him. That day she buried his little three-year-old body in her sister's garden and said goodbye that way. By her own admission, it didn't make her heart feel any better.

A few weeks later, still heartbroken, Karen prayed to God and her guardian angel for a sign that her little one was okay and that he knew he had been loved. She was thinking of Clyde as she drove along the rural countryside. As she did so, the radio suddenly played the song 'Spirit in the Sky' by Doctor and the Medics. Karen explained that as she listened to the lyrics, she knew it was a sign from God. It really made her day.

Strangely, that song has come up in numerous reader experiences over the years. I wonder if the lyricist had any idea how comforting the words would be to so many people!

* * *

Dogs in Heaven

Jess first wrote to me a long time ago now, but her story stuck in my mind. She explained that she and her mum were talking in her bedroom. She was sitting on the bed and her mum was kneeling on the floor. Ruby the cat was curled up by her mum's legs, sleeping, and as the pair were chatting, her mum suddenly shot bolt upright. Her eyes filled with shock and then tears. Jess said she immediately panicked and wondered what had happened. When her mum finally got her words out, she explained that she'd started stroking the cat by her side and only after a few seconds did it register that Ruby was curled up on her other side! She swore that the cat she stroked was physically there – she could feel the fur, the body, everything. The pair decided that it must have been Gladys, another family cat who'd passed on when Jess was nineteen. Both women felt confident that Gladys had simply jumped at the opportunity to say hello from the other side.

Jess explained that, in hindsight, it probably wasn't as unexpected as they first thought. Previously, three people, including herself, had seen a cat run downstairs and under the table (where Gladys was found before being put to sleep at the vets), and even felt her climbing on the bed. The family miss their old cat terribly, but feel grateful that she still appears from time to time – even if it gives them a shock!

June explained to me that her son had a black cat called Freddie (named after June's dad, who'd passed

35

away in 1998). Freddie had been with the family since he was a kitten and her son seemed to treat him like a dog. Freddie even did as he was told (and let's face it, cats don't normally do that!).

The years rolled by and as June's son moved to a busy area, she adopted Freddie. Sadly, two years ago Freddie died, but June says she still feels his presence around her – sometimes she even glimpses him out of the corner of her eye. One day, when June's son was visiting, he called out to his mum that he'd seen his old pet in the house. What a comfort to think that Freddie had come to say goodbye to him! Over time Freddie's visits became less frequent, but it was wonderful to know that the connection between the family and their pet remained unbroken.

Jan also wrote to me many years ago. I included one of her stories in another book but kept this one on file in case I had the opportunity to use it. She explained how she'd been feeding and looking after a feral cat for a long while. It lived in the garden and slept in a kennel they'd built, but Jan was sad because the cat, whom they named Saffron (Saffie), remained wild and wouldn't come into the house. Saffie was beautiful – a tortoiseshell cat with pretty markings.

One day Jan became so frustrated at the cat's lack of trust in her that she grabbed a photograph of her late son and asked him to make Saffie tame. Jan says that she regularly spoke to her son like that because it made her feel closer to him since her loss. The very next morning something unusual happened. A strange cat walked into the conservatory; it wore a collar with a bell and seemed so friendly. This new cat followed Jan all round the house, and every time she put it out it came back in again, purring and sitting on her lap. It even followed her into the bathroom!

Jan took the new cat down to the local vet to have it checked out and to see if anybody had posted an advert saying they had lost one. Rather bizarrely, it turned out that the inquisitive cat belonged to the vet herself, and she'd lost it a year earlier! The vet asked if Jan would like to keep it, because she was in the process of moving to London. The cat was named Spuddie, and Jan immediately adopted him as her own. This isn't the end of the story, though. The new cat seems to have given the old one confidence. Saffie now comes in for all of her meals and is happy to spend time with Jan. She firmly believes her son intervened from the other side, answering her plea for help!

Chapter 3

Animals Are Humans?

One of the most unusual phenomena relating to the afterlife is when humans come back from the other side ... as animals! I'm not sure if your great-uncle becomes a butterfly or if he just borrows a butterfly body for a brief moment. Is the robin tapping on your window really your grandma, or is it just a robin passing on a message? The many such stories I've received over the years make me believe that there is great truth in this idea.

All over the world there are customs that indicate it may be possible for this to happen. The early Christians saw the butterfly as a soul, for example; in some parts of England it was believed that the butterfly contained the spirit of a child returned from the dead. Some shamans train their spirit to temporarily enter the body of an animal. They use the experience to gain wisdom and spiritual growth.

My postbag has contained numerous stories over the years of people noticing birds acting in unusual ways after a loss. In the UK robins have become symbols of loved ones popping back from the other side to reassure their human grievers that they are happy and safe in their new heavenly home. In other parts of the world stories of magpies, owls and hummingbirds have contained the essence of this belief. You may well have experienced other animals, especially wild creatures or animals you particularly associated with the deceased.

Some people have shared stories in which they feel a loved one has (initially, at least) returned to the family in the body of a new kitten or puppy, to continue sharing their lives with the family they love.

Sometimes owners believe that the spirit of a deceased pet resides in their new family pet (of the same or a different species). I once had a dream that the spirit of my dog Lady had returned as my new black kitten. I had no particular proof that this was the case, and certainly the kitten had a more mischievous and confident personality than Lady! Prior to that, I was 'told' in another dream that Lady was the reincarnation of a dog my family had owned when I was a child – Candy, the one who was vicious and bit my face, splitting my lip. I needed stitches. As before, the personalities of the two pets were dramatically different, and they didn't feel like the same soul. Maybe it was just a weird dream, but somehow I'm not so sure! My 'dreams' showed that the same pet returned to me three times: twice as dogs and then finally as a cat.

I wasn't keen on the nasty-tempered Candy, but certainly loved the second incarnation as Lady. By the time she returned as Magik, the cat (her third female form), I adored her. She was a constant companion, always sitting close by. Regular followers of my work will remember reading about her in many of my magazine columns, articles and features, and in several of my books. She even received her own fan mail. In her final lifetime with us (of just seven short years), she'd certainly got things right and left her own legacy as well as a great sadness in my heart. Perhaps animals, like humans, return to live many lifetimes, each time growing as a soul, evolving in their own way.

In her book *Animals in Spirit: Our Faithful Companions' Transition to the Afterlife*, Penelope Smith writes about why she feels that animal spirits might return again to the same family in the body of a new pet. She describes how pets might feel as if they hadn't had enough time to complete their life mission with their owner and therefore welcomed the opportunity of more time. As an animal communicator she explained how one seventeen-year-old cat felt it needed to help enlighten its owner. Yet we think *we* are the ones with all the answers! Maybe we've had it wrong all this time; our pets may be the enlightened ones, who work with us on earth as our dear companions and guides. And maybe if they don't reincarnate they continue to work with us from the other side of life. I'm sure they do.

My dear friend Jenny Smedley, the bestselling author, was kind enough to share her story with me so I could include it here. Jenny has written several books about animals, and she told me about the extraordinary events that led her to her new puppy. 'When I stared down at the puppy, spread-eagled on her back in my arms,' she said, 'it was like she grinned up at me.' Jenny wondered if the puppy in her arms could really be her old dog, come back to her in a new body.

When her wonderful soulmate dog Ace got old, Jenny lived in dread of saying goodbye to her. Ace was a big black Labrador and German Shepherd cross, and Jenny loved her like a child. When she was twelve years old, Ace had gone through the trauma of having a mammary tumour removed from her stomach, losing a nipple in the process, but her indomitable spirit had pulled her through.

Inevitably, though, the dreaded time came when Ace was fifteen. The once lively and proud dog had become a shadow of her former self, and despite agonising over the decision, Jenny knew it would be cruel to let her struggle on just because she didn't want to lose her. Jenny was devastated at the loss of her beloved Ace and thought she'd never get over it. Like many owners she decided she was *never, ever* going through that again. No more dogs would mean no more heartache! But Ace had other plans.

Later that year Jenny and her husband, Tony, took a trip to Sedona in Arizona, a magical, stunning place. On 13 September, while they were away, she had a reading with a psychic. The woman knew nothing about her except her name. Despite this, it was a very good and accurate reading. At the end the psychic asked her if she had any questions. Jenny took the opportunity to ask if she had any messages from her parents, both passed over. 'No,' the psychic replied, 'but I have a message from your dog.' She then went on to describe a big black dog with grey whiskers (Ace had been very grey around her face by the time she'd died). The message was: 'Today I'm young again.' At first Jenny thought the message meant her late dog was now rejuvenated in the spirit realm, but later she understood the deeper meaning.

After returning from their trip, Jenny spotted an advertisement in the local paper for some puppies at a nearby farm that were in need of a new home. Jenny noticed that the puppies had been born on 13 September, the day Ace had told the psychic that she was young again. Curiosity forced her to go and look, so Jenny and Tony made an appointment up at the big old farmhouse to see the puppies. They were a Springer Spaniel/Labrador cross.

As the back door opened, a stream of black and white puppies poured out into the sunshine – all of them except one. A small black bitch puppy made a beeline for the couple. She clambered up into Jenny's arms, and the farmer said, 'That's odd. She's usually a bit shy, that one.' The puppy had wriggled in her arms, baring her belly for a tickle. As she did so, Jenny stared in astonishment. There, plain to see, was a blank space where one of her nipples should have been. Her perfect pink tummy was just smooth in that spot. Just as Ace had been missing a nipple when she died, this puppy had been born with a nipple missing too. Right away Jenny realised this was no coincidence. Ace had come back, and the couple called her KC.

The strange phenomenon was corroborated a while later by the psychic. Unasked, and knowing nothing of what had happened, she sent Jenny a drawing of a puppy – clearly KC – and told her it had been sent to her by a black German Shepherd and Labrador cross, who'd told her, 'This is me now.' The part of Ace's soul that was still in spirit had sent her the ultimate sign …

When Hay House publishers offered Jenny the chance to research and write a book specifically about the existence of pet souls, she was delighted. As her book took shape she was astounded by the thousands of stories sent to her about incidences that again proved animals are really no different from us.

Jenny now believes that pets do have souls, are capable of love and also of reason. They have been shown to make decisions that put their owner's safety above their own, and have most certainly returned from the spirit world after their death to bring comfort and solace to their bereaved owners. My dear friend, like me, is a firm believer!

A lady called Angela told me another story about how her son communicated with her after he had passed away. She had ten years of messages from him (various signs from the other side), but one of her strongest memories is when a magpie was tapping on her bedroom window, just after his funeral.

Bird stories like this are really commonplace. Birds can act extra-friendly at times, but it's the timing of the experiences that makes them so special. Glenys recalls how her father always used to joke that when he died he was going to come back as a crow. He said he'd be happy to sit on the fence if someone threw him a little something every now and again. Glenys says that she likes to throw scraps out each day, and the food seems to be mainly taken by a regular visitor … a black crow! This mysterious crow also tends to turn up at important family occasions. I'm sure that a bird would be less scary than a full manifestation of a deceased loved one appearing at the dining-room table, whatever we might think.

One very clever man made sure his daughter saw his name in a pet cemetery and made full use of their horse connection to show her that he was still around

… but let me start from the beginning and share the whole story with you.

Rosie wrote to tell me that her dad, Roy, had passed away two months before. Sadly, this lovely man had mouth cancer, which kept coming back despite increasingly aggressive and debilitating treatments. She was with her father right up until the minutes before he died (she believes he waited until she left the room before passing away). She was so grateful that she had the opportunity to tell him that she loved him and was proud of him. Rosie knew her dad was dying and whispered that it was okay for him to go, knowing it was time for him to leave for his new home in heaven.

Rosie misses her dad horribly and says she has really struggled to cope with his loss. But then, a couple of weeks after he died, she says there was a period when she kept finding white feathers everywhere. There seemed to be a pattern to them; they usually manifested themselves when she was particularly upset or talking about her dad. Eventually, she asked for an unmistakable sign that it wasn't just a coincidence, and when she lifted her daughter out of the bath, there was a white feather on top of her head, tucked in her hair!

Soon, though, Rosie began doubting again. A few days before she wrote to me, she spoke out loud that the feathers could have come from anywhere or anyone, and said, 'If it's really you, Dad, show me horses, let me know it's you.' (Horses are animals that she associates with her dad.) The next day, while reading one of my books on her e-reader, she noticed an advertisement at the end for a book about a war horse, with a picture of a horse on it. She immediately wondered if this was a sign. Then, not long after, she and her husband decided to go with their family to a nearby castle, but her husband changed his mind at the last minute and so they visited Brodsworth Hall instead. Strangely, inside the stately home there are many paintings of horses. One room in particular is covered in nothing but; 'There must have been thirty horse paintings in that room alone!' Rosie told me.

Quietly she said, 'Okay, Dad, but show me you're really here. Show me your name written down – just your first name will do.' Then the family went out into the gardens. At one point, Rosie says, she spotted a little path and could just make out some small stones alongside it that resembled gravestones. Rosie felt drawn towards them and wandered off alone. It was a pet cemetery. The first few graves were marked 'Cuddles', 'Faithful friend', 'Polly the parrot', and the like, with dates underneath. Rosie was shocked at what she saw next. Turning to the second row, the first headstone had the word 'Roy' engraved upon it! Her dad's first name, written down just like she'd asked for! Oh, and apparently there were white feathers – thousands of them – all over the grounds.

Dogs in Heaven

Did Rosie's dad suddenly appear in the image of a horse, or even create the name on the cemetery plaque? No, it's unlikely, but spirits are sneaky things. This loving dad did whatever he could to bring comfort to the daughter he adored, and made full use of the animal connection he was known for by drawing the family towards what they needed to see. Not having believed in an afterlife before, this woman quickly became a believer. As she says 'If it's all just been a series of coincidences, then it's astonishing!' It is indeed!

Chapter 4

Mystical Encounters and Paranormal Experiences

Stories of pets living after death and even reincarnating to return to the same owners are very peculiar indeed. It all seems impossible to believe, but when I tell you that what you've read here is just the tip of the iceberg, it's because I've been sent many other stories of animals and the paranormal.

This next story that I came across is particularly odd. When a dog was hit by a car, he sadly had to be put down. Strangely, the place on the road where he'd been hit seems to have retained the energy of the dog. When local riders came to the area afterwards, their horses refused to go anywhere near the spot, almost as if part of the dog and its tragedy was still held there. Animals, so used to relying on their instincts, may be more likely to pick up on these energies than humans.

Johanna is an animal communicator and 'speaks' to animals using telepathy. It's quite a special psychic skill. I know several people who do this and most of them fell upon the ability, not knowing how it came about or where it came from. For others, the ability began following a serious illness or near-death experience. Being so close to death seems to jumpstart many people's psychic abilities.

Johanna shares a house with her cat, Buffy. Johanna first met Buffy when she appeared in a type of vision, in which the cat announced that she was going to come to her. Then, a few weeks later, the ginger cat appeared in another vision and said, 'I'm here, you'd better come and get me.' Johanna was confused and wondered where her new cat was located! At the time she was doing a veterinary nurse course and was assigned to do work experience for a local vet. On his door was a sign: 'Free to a good home. Ginger kitten.' The 'ginger kitten' was Buffy, of course, and Johanna took her new pet home.

Isn't it strange how we are under the illusion that we select our pet? Johanna's story reminded me of my own, when my cat first appeared to me in a dream and then to my daughter, showing the connection to the butterfly. Clearly our pets choose us!

Many of you will know that, these days, a white feather is a recognised 'calling card' of the angels, which commonly appears as a sign that our deceased loved ones are around us. I've filled many chapters of my books with angel feather stories, but I love that this next one features a pet. Fiona wrote about an experience that included her dog, a retriever (which, amusingly, Fiona swears never retrieves anything normally!). One day, she was walking her dog in a flooded field and as she did so she was thinking about her recently departed father. Her dog went bounding off to the deepest part of the flood and dropped his prize at her feet. The dog had retrieved a white feather! Isn't that funny? The word angel means messenger, but in this case it seems like the dog was the angel between worlds, passing on a very welcome sign.

When Elaine started working full-time, she quickly realised it wasn't fair on her little dog Chloe. It seemed that the kindest thing to do would be to find someone who would be able to spend more time with her. Elaine told me that a friend at work had a little boy who was desperate for a dog and would take Chloe. Elaine handed over her pet for the weekend and Chloe immediately settled in. Her loving owner still wasn't sure what to do. She so wanted her dog to be happy, but also knew she would miss her a great deal. Believing in a higher power, Elaine thought she'd ask the angels to bring her some sort of message. She asked, 'If I'm doing the right thing, Archangel Michael, please send me a sign!'

Three days passed and nothing happened, but then on the fourth day she went outside to empty the bins and there in the sky for all the world to see was a huge sword formed by the clouds! Michael, of course, is well known as the warrior angel, and in statues and paintings always carries his flaming sword. Chloe went to live with Elaine's work colleague and had another six years of happiness.

Chapter 5

Clever Pets

I am always surprised at how many stories I find about pets grieving for the loss of their owners. I was fascinated by the account of the twelve-year-old German Shepherd who'd taken to visiting the church his owner attended before she died. The dog, named Ciccio, started to turn up at the Santa Maria Assunta church in Italy every day after his mistress died. The faithful pet arrived at the church when the bells rang and even sat at the altar throughout the service. Locals brought him food and water because they were so impressed by his loyal behaviour. The story is similar to Bobby, a Skye Terrier, who was well known for sitting at his owner's grave at the Greyfriars Kirkyard cemetery in Edinburgh. One wonders if the pets realise their owners have passed away, or if they are hoping that by following such rituals their owners will reappear. Maybe, as many believe, they are simply honouring the human loved ones they have lost.

In another heartbreaking story, a faithful canine named Hachiko hung around the train station where his owner had died – he appeared for many years afterwards. And when an eighteen-year-old boy was tragically killed, his pet – a brown mongrel he had once rescued – sat by his grave for several weeks, refusing to eat. Eventually, people managed to tempt the dog away, and he went on to live with the deceased boy's grieving mother.

When Tommy's owner passed away in a car accident, the loyal dog stayed at his grave for fifteen days. When rescuers approached they swore the dog was shedding tears. These are just a few of the stories I've found during my research. Sad though they are, no one could doubt the connection between these pets and their owners. Why should animals be any different to humans? With a bond so close, why wouldn't pets pop back from heaven if they could?

Can animals save our lives? I've discovered numerous stories where owners believed this had been the case. After much investigation I felt that in some of the cases the pet may have accidentally saved the family's life, but in other stories the pet may well have intervened in an intelligent way. What do you think of these?

The Noble family were in the news after their fridge-freezer caught fire in the middle of the night. The parents and three children were fast asleep when the fire started, and the smoke alarm, which had been tested just two weeks earlier, failed to alert them.

Luckily, the Nobles' seven-year-old Bengal cat Simba began mewing loudly, trying to attract the attention of his owners. Thankfully, he woke mum Caroline up and the family all escaped the house in the nick of time, taking heroic Simba with them. Caroline later described the house as being 'as hot as a sauna', and the whole family felt they owed their lives to their clever cat.

In another story, a two-year-old pit bull named Ace was also hailed a hero after saving the life of his deaf owner, by similarly alerting him to the fire that had broken out in his home.

Shocks the donkey suffered terrible abuse at the hands of his owner, being deliberately dowsed in bleach. After his dreadful ordeal vets nursed him back to health, but the horror of his experience left him fragile, and he found it difficult to cope in the donkey rescue centre that wanted to care for him.

Over time this beautiful creature was helped in his recovery by caring for others; Shocks is now a therapy donkey, giving rides to disabled children and those in need. Although not life-saving, it was certainly life-enhancing for both the animal and the humans involved, and this partnership meant that Shocks went on to win the title of 2013 Rescue Animal of the Year.

While watching television one evening, a woman was terrified when a masked intruder burst into her home carrying a gun. The gunman's intent was to rob the home, but the family pet – a rescue dog named Mariah – growled and chased the thief out of the house. Her owner calls her pet her saviour!

We get cross when our dogs bark too much, but their instinct to protect us from danger is great. The loyalty they share with us means that a dog never seems too afraid to put their own life ahead of ours.

Then there is the story of Davide, on a day in the year 2000 that he will never forget. When Davide – a non-swimmer – fell from his father's fishing boat into the sea off the Adriatic coast, his father was unaware at first that his son was missing. The boy was spotted by Filippo, a wild dolphin. Filippo is a bit of a tourist attraction off Manfredonia in south-east Italy. The friendly creature quickly swam in to conduct a rescue, pushing the boy up out of the water to stop him drowning. The boy grabbed hold of the dolphin, who pushed him right up against the boat so he was close enough for his father to pull him back aboard. The dolphin had been a familiar sight in the area after becoming separated from a visiting school of dolphins a couple of years earlier. He seemed unafraid of humans, and completely understood that the boy had been in trouble!

Todd would understand this only too well. He was out surfing when a 15-foot great white shark suddenly appeared out of nowhere. In no time at all, the shark had bitten Todd's torso, pinning him to his surfboard, before grabbing hold of his leg. Todd explained how at this point a pod of bottlenose dolphins appeared and began circling him, keeping the shark away.

No one knows quite why these creatures protect humans, but, according to the Whale and Dolphin Conservation Society, there are stories of such rescues that go right back to Ancient Greece. There is a similar story from 2004 in New Zealand of four lifeguards being rescued from a shark by dolphins in the same way.

I loved dog owner Brenda's experience. When she was taking Penny, her ten-year-old dog, on her regular walk she spotted an empty wheelchair by the side of the river. Brenda looked down the bank and spotted a woman drowning in the river below. Brenda called to her clever pet to 'Fetch!' and without a second's hesitation the dog dived in and dragged the woman out of the water to safety! Even though a human is more difficult to 'fetch' than a rubber ball, the dog completely understood the command and went on to rescue the unlucky (or lucky) person in the river.

When this next experience became public I don't think there was a dry eye anywhere. James Crane worked in the World Trade Centre – right up on the 101st floor. Every day he took his golden retriever Daisy with him, James's support and guide dog for the blind.

Dogs in Heaven

On 11 September 2001, when the plane hit the tower several floors below where James worked, he felt that his own life had ended already. In a final act of mercy he let Daisy go, and she disappeared into the smoke-filled building. Along with many others that day, James was just waiting to die as smoke and fumes from the jet choked the air.

Bizarrely, half an hour later, Daisy appeared back at her owner's side, and she had brought James's boss with her. Daisy had guided him down from eleven floors above. The canine heroine led James and his boss out of the building, along with 300 other people. Knowing that more people were caught up in the smoke and fumes, Daisy – against her owner's wishes – ran back inside and rescued hundreds more people. On her third run the building collapsed, and her grief-stricken owner fell to his knees in tears.

Unbelievably, Daisy survived, although this time she was carried out by a firefighter. The fireman explained how the life-saving animal had led firefighters right to where people were trapped. She'd been badly burned on her paws and had a broken leg, but all in all she saved nearly a thousand lives. Mayor Giuliani himself awarded Daisy the New York City's Medal of Honor! I hope she was treated to a steak as well, bless her.

I was fascinated to read the news story of the dog that saved a boy from a swarm of bees, which certainly shows intent to save. The Oregon boy was out playing when he stood on a log and unwittingly released the mass of bees. They swarmed around him and his older sister. Both children were stung over and over again, and, scarily, his sister had a bee allergy. Covered in bees and stings, the boy was unable to make it back to the house to call for help.

Luckily, though, help came to them. The family dog, another pit bull, named Hades, dragged the young boy up onto some grass before allowing the boy to crawl onto her back so she could carry him to his mother! The dog was also stung several times, and all three needed treatment, with both children being rushed to the local hospital. They all survived to tell the tale, and the dog was designated the family champion. Isn't that amazing?

Animals can save our lives in more subtle ways. For example, there is definitely a scientific connection between our emotions and our health, and existing research shows how living with pets and having animals as part of our lives makes us healthier. Any pet owner already knows this startling piece of scientific discovery already. They calm us when we are agitated – stroking them soothes both them and us – and always make us feel better.

Have you ever had an experience like these? I lost one of my dear cats earlier this year and I was devastated. I haven't had a sign from Magik yet, but at least I was able to memorialise her. I was creating a pack of divination cards at the time (cards used for inspirational readings called 'Messages from Heaven'), and we used her image on one of them. It helped me a lot. I also kept her collar and hung it on a toy cat. It comforts me, although my other cat Tigger was completely freaked out the first time he heard the bell ring after Magik died. Bless him! I guess he thought she had come back from the dead.

When my dog Lady died, Tigger was quite depressed for several weeks. He seemed to understand that his companion wasn't coming home. Our pets have a greater understanding of these things than we could possibly imagine. As well as experiencing their own distress, they seem to pick up our thoughts and feelings on the matter as well. They also need lots of hugs and attention to help them get through the grief. Many recommend bringing a dead pet home or taking the living pet to see the deceased animal. This gives them the opportunity to understand the process.

Many people find it useful to create memorials for their pets after they have passed on. In a previous book I suggested creating a book of memories (if your pet is still around, make sure you record special days by keeping a note of them or taking regular photographs). You might decide to get a special portrait done (perhaps a photo-sitting, or a painting or artist's drawing using an existing photograph).

How about dedicating a special part of the garden to them, or buying or making a memorial plaque or figurine (the Internet is a wonderful source of such objects). When my little black cat passed on my husband bought me a black lacquered cat hook for my tea-towels! It sounds daft, but it hangs usefully in the kitchen and I find it's a fun reminder. You could also build a website in their honour or maybe find a way to help other grieving owners. Why not raise some funds in their name for a special charity? All these things can help to bring meaning to your pet's life. The most important thing, of course, is to remember every day how much your pet means to you right now. Enjoy every minute of the time you have together – no regrets!

Our pets are the most amazing gifts from heaven. They love us in life and watch over us in death. We feel that we have selected them to live with us when the truth is, it may well be the other way round. We feel that we help and look after our animals, but as we have seen, they do the same for us. As humans we feel we are superior, but it seems that God's creatures are just as wise. They have the capacity to love in a way that few humans ever can.

I've felt privileged to be able to compile this collection of animal stories for you, and I hope that it makes you feel a little closer to your own pets, both those on this side of life and those we have lost. Of course, when I say 'lost', you know I mean that they never really leave us. Like humans, their spirits move on to another – and some say better – place. I hope, like me, you are lucky enough to have a visit from pets of your own once they have crossed over to the afterlife.

If you have already had an experience like this then I'd love to hear about it. And if you've enjoyed this short read, please feel free to check out some of my others.

Until we meet again,
Much love,
Jacky Newcomb
'The Angel Lady' x

www.JackyNewcomb.com

Harper True.
Time to be inspired

Write for us

Do you have a true life story of your own?

Whether you think it will inspire us move us, make us laugh or make us cry, we want to hear from you.

To find out more, visit

www.harpertrue.com or send your ideas to harpertrue@harpercollins.co.uk and soon you could be a published author.